12/15/93

DEAN CHRISTENSEN,

I hope you will accept this small token of appreciation from your colleagues in the Design Department. With it comes a sincere gesture of appreciation for the great work you are doing in our and for the rest of the Colleges' behalf.

We are looking forward to a continued positive relationship.

Thanks again,

Robert Barrett
The Design Department

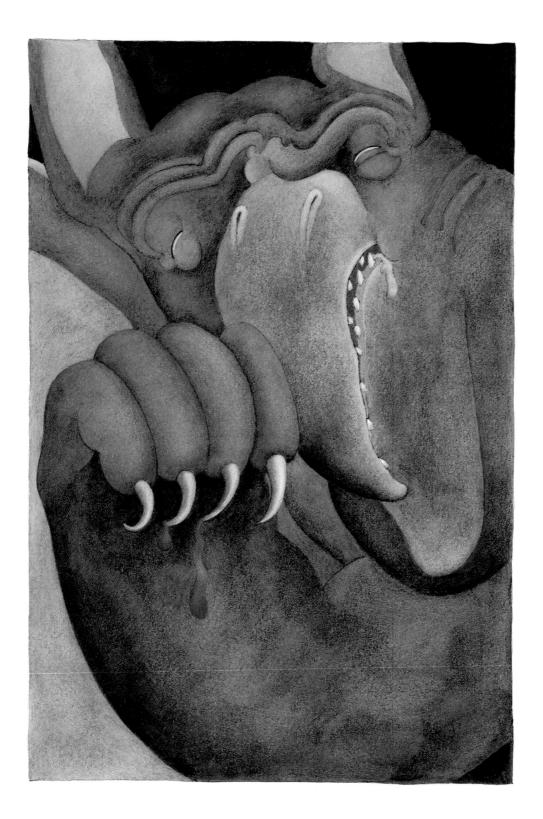

ETIENNE
·DELESSERT·

DESIGNED BY RITA MARSHALL

STEWART, TABORI & CHANG
NEW YORK

Text copyright ©1991 Stewart, Tabori & Chang, Inc.
Illustrations copyright ©1991 Etienne Delessert

Published in 1992 by Stewart, Tabori & Chang, Inc.
575 Broadway, New York, New York 10012
Published simultaneously in French by Editions Gallimard

Library of Congress Cataloging-in-Publication Data
Etienne Delessert/designed by Rita Marshall.
p.   cm.
Includes bibliographical references.
ISBN 1-55670-224-8
1.Delessert, Etienne—Appreciation. I.Marshall, Rita.
NC988.5.D45E8   1992   91-16661
741.6′092—dc20   CIP

Distributed in the U.S. by Workman Publishing,
708 Broadway, New York, New York 10003
Distributed in Canada by Canadian Manda Group,
P.O. Box 920 Station U, Toronto, Ontario M8Z 5P9
Distributed in all other territories by
Little, Brown and Company, International Division,
34 Beacon Street, Boston, Massachusetts 02108

Printed in Japan
10 9 8 7 6 5 4 3 2 1

Page 2: Beauty and the Beast, watercolor, 1984
Page 3: Il était une Fois la Souris, ink, 1977
Page 5: Indians, Pétrole Progrès Magazine, gouache, 1966

▲ I met Etienne twenty-five years ago in a magazine. I was struck by his picture of four native Americans sitting in a car dressed in their best ornamentation, their feathers bright with Etienne's colors. Since then I have seen his drawings and paintings in books and magazines, galleries and museums. In them, life and death meet, prophets and monsters battle. But for me, Etienne is still the Indian I met twenty-five years ago.

P IERRE M ARCHAND

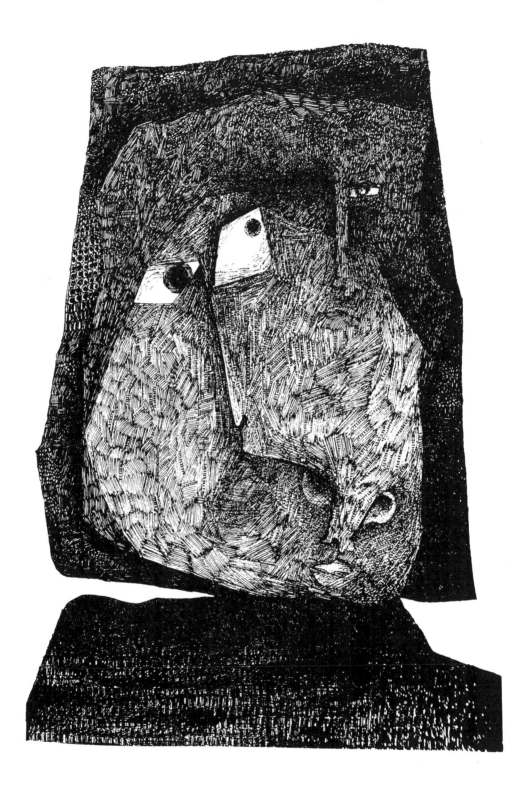

KAFKA CONTRE L'ABSURDE INK 1962

· 6 ·

The name Etienne Delessert came up in a conversation in 1960, early in my career as a publisher, when I was on the lookout for books that would embody the aesthetics of the new and promising decade. Then, in the garden of a mutual friend, where Etienne had spent so many hours of his childhood holidays, I met the young, unknown nineteen-year-old. I was struck at once by the unusual intensity of his awareness, his intelligence, and his strong opinions.

IN THE REAL WORLD, AS IN HIS TALES, ETIENNE WAS POSSESSED BY A PASSION FOR PEOPLE. HIS VISION BROKE THEM DOWN INTO GROTESQUES AND RAISED THEM TO THE LEVEL OF MYTH.

■ The young apprentice graphic artist, who had just passed his Baccalauréat examination in Lausanne, where we were both living at the time, had had a classical education, including Greek and Latin. He was now eager, however, to abandon traditional paths, sever past links, and strike out on his own. He had rejected the idea of a university education and did not want to attend art school. Not that he was interested in isolating himself, like so many young creative people; on the contrary, he wanted to get down into the vast marketplace of world communications as quickly as he could. One sensed from the fervor of his blue-eyed gaze that this young man believed with all his heart in the power of the individual. He believed in the existence of great and unique creators.

● From the very beginning I had sensed the clarity of his ambition. As we discussed details, he was already putting them into perspective, situating them within his integrated universe of traditional painting, magazine illustration, advertising, and new printing techniques.

▲ The young Etienne had grown up reading all the usual stories about Ben Hur, Robin Hood, and Selma Lagerlöf's Nils Holgersson. He had never shown much interest in coloring books, but at the age of twelve, pictures suddenly began to crowd his mind, taking precedence over his taste for words. He began to observe, to imagine, to have odd and precise dreams. He now added Max Bill, Neue Grafik posters, and grown-up modern art to Walt Disney, Père Castor, and the animal books illustrated by Rojankovsky, which had delighted his childhood. Etienne seemed impatient to draw his own world, but his naive technical ignorance forced him to proceed with precision. The "how" always prevailed over the "what." His imagination readily came up with subjects, but he then had to create his own methods for realizing them.

■ Etienne had enrolled in an accelerated internship course at the studio of a graphic artist in Lausanne, but he refused to do the formal classwork that was required. His painter friends in the local avant garde were shocked at his overt interest in commissions and his desire to communicate with his clients. Etienne's goal was to gain an exact understanding of the idea he wanted to express, and in order to formulate it he engaged in various visual experiments. Was he selling out? Hardly. He regarded advertising, magazines, book or record jackets, as natural aesthetic opportunities—the artistic battlegrounds of his era—and as a means of depicting, with the help of money miraculously contributed by others, his own world, his own characters, and his own cosmogony.

● He discovered the outstanding illustrators in GRAPHIS, the international magazine out of Zurich, but noted that after a period of intense inspiration, Swiss graphic art had started to run out of steam. He began to look further afield for innovation—to Paris, the United States, and Japan.

▲ At the age of nineteen, Etienne was wary of the closed world of provincial art, although he did admire some of the well-known painters of his native land, those who had demonstrated a stubborn independence in their work. One of them was Lausanne's René Auberjonois, who had spent years unlearning what the Ecole des Beaux-Arts had taught him. His example served to strengthen the young creator's burning desire for autonomy.

■ At the time I met him, his self-assurance was already clearly evident. I also came to recognize, however, the generosity that was a part of his controlling personality, a generosity that made him listen intently to other people's stories and to enter into their problems with warm sympathy, imaginatively, giving advice that one ignored at the risk of incurring his wrath.

● In the real world, as in his tales, Etienne was possessed by a passion for people. His vision broke them down into grotesques and raised them to the level of myth. Like a Creator, he breathed life into his creatures; his ideas always became incarnate. Both his synthesizing mind and his capacity for work impelled his art toward a baroque universality.

▲ The young graphic artist was the son of a pastor, little influenced by the Gospels but nourished, like Friedrich Dürrenmatt, by the Old Testament,

with its picturesque prophets. As a child, Etienne was fond of animals and flowers, which came to exemplify grace and paradise in his work. Over the years, I have seen many *bonshommes* in the illustrator's half-fantastic, half-real landscapes, where one is surprised now by devils, now by animals straight out of the Garden of Eden.

■ He solved the problem of graphics for my own books in a trice, devising for them a brilliant white cover, the upper half of which was always blank. For several years, that bright white rectangle symbolized my publishing house. As if paying a tribute to his classical education, the black titles were printed in rigorously elegant Bodoni. His work, which concerned even the smallest detail of texture and typography, made him much more than a mere graphic artist working on commission. He was a conscience—and a bad conscience, should anyone's creative ambition and desire for perfection slacken. And, as is obvious, he also became a friend and accomplice. He was able to capture the spirit of a book before even reading it. He got to know the writers we began to publish. His personality and his influence were inextricably bound up with the literary enterprise that was to transform the climate of French Switzerland over the next twenty years.

● Etienne's work was not confined to layout. One of the first books we undertook was an essay on Kafka, and Etienne illustrated it. He recognized the author of THE CASTLE as a master. The young high-school graduate from Lausanne had never learned to draw, and he now set out to create a style and technique for himself. His first ink drawings—Kafka's portrait as a man crushed by the absurd and a burrow—possess a line, a compositional

strength, and a metaphysical message that time has not weakened. They presage the painter beneath the graphic artist. Later, he was to write: "In Kafka I found the wealth of an invented world." Etienne instinctively preferred the writer who wrote of breakdown and decay to the Greco-Roman models his education had set for him. He was drawn to the shadowy elements in Kafka's work and became aware of his own affinities with Central Europe, and with Jewish Expressionism, with the fantasies and phantasms amid which his perception of reality blossomed.

▲ During the 1960s many painters were taken aback by the rising prices in the art world and the recourse to every imaginable style. One technique seemed to be doing battle with another. But, from the very beginning the young man from Lausanne was fueled by a huge appetite for synthesis. Working on his first assignment for a publishing house, he wanted to share in all my concerns. He was constantly glowing with ideas—for some typographical decoration, for an advertising campaign, for a strategic decision, or a suggestion for a new book. It was his passion, no matter how much effort it cost. Thus we collaborated in frequent meetings over the course of three or four years, until his trips to Paris—quickly followed by further success—became more and more frequent. And then he was off to New York. He set out alone, without—to my surprise—knowing a word of English, but, as ever, with the spirit of the conqueror.

BERTIL GALLAND

1964. When Bayard Presse was planning to launch FORMIDABLE, a monthly magazine for teenagers, Albert Hollenstein, one of the pioneers in new-wave print media, sent us a youthful art director. His name was Etienne Delessert. He was Swiss, appropriately opinionated and meticulous, and just the counterbalance needed for the somewhat extravagant enthusiasm of the editorial team.

▲ Then came the months of dummy copies and mock-ups. All of us worked together, crammed into a small, grimy office. Anyone who has ever put out a new publication will recall those extraordinary days when everything seems possible, but when the dream seems to slip away like sand between your fingers once an idea is transformed into real, tangible pages. The gold nugget you thought you had found turns out to be a rough stone that you must laboriously smooth and polish.

■ You, Etienne, didn't shrink from long, work-filled nights and weekends of study, or from redoing a layout ten times just because a tenth of a millimeter of blank space bothered you. One morning you came up with a suggestion, a slight modification in the title. You wanted to change FORMIDABLE to FORMIDIABLE. Somewhere in a cupboard I must still have your layout of the title, with the little devil dotting the second "i." Were you pulling our leg? I'm not so sure.

● Then the first issue was almost ready. We had decided to feature a young singer, Sylvie Vartan, on the cover. You made some huge paper daisies,

THE CHILDREN'S AUDIENCE IS NO SMALL THING. TO THE CONTRARY. THEY DEMAND FURTHER AND GREATER EFFORT, AND EVEN MORE HONESTY, FOR THEY CANNOT DEFEND THEMSELVES, AND EVERYTHING WE CREATE FOR THEM HAS AN IMPACT ON THE REST OF THEIR LIVES.

and we watched as you and the flowers set out for the photographer's studio in a little green Triumph. You didn't make it. An accident, the hospital, and then a lengthy convalescence. The daisies were more resilient than you and were used in the photograph: an early indication of your work's durability.

▲ That was our first encounter. Thirty years have now gone by. Your work has been abundant and rich, but it is still marked by tension between God and the Devil, the force of evil and the gentleness of Heaven.

■ 1970. Jacqueline Joubert, the director of programming for French television, wanted to create a series in France comparable to America's "Sesame Street." She asked our team to come up with a weekly, twenty-four-minute television program for her. A month later, we showed her our project. Joubert was encouraging, but she thought our plan needed an animated segment. Where, in those days and at a price that Radio-Television Française could afford, were we going to find an animated segment that would have the graphic and pedagogical tone of the rest of the program? One of the draftsmen said to me: "You should look in Switzerland. There's a young man there with a lot of talent who has just done a few very impressive segments for "Sesame Street.""

● Telephone call after telephone call. Then, suddenly, six years after FORMIDABLE, I again heard Etienne Delessert's voice.

▲ Two days later you were in Paris and had joined

us in the long journey of "Tic et Tac, Toc et Poule." Many laborious months passed before we finally came up with a really fine pilot. And did we show it! Was there a television program director in the world or an editor who attended the Bologna or Frankfurt fairs who didn't see it? Christian Gallimard and Pierre Marchand came to every showing and supported us wholeheartedly, both during and afterwards. And we needed it, because the equation was a simple one: production costs of sixty thousand francs per minute against an acquisition budget of one thousand francs a minute for any French—or European—television channel.

■ We were faced with the fact that we couldn't survive without the American market. You knew that market, and together we laid siege to it. ABC had been wanting to develop a program that could compete with "Sesame Street" and liked our project. Things started to gel. They even began to firm up. We were on the point of signing when, at the very last minute, the U.S. government passed a law limiting the time given to advertising before, during, and after any program aimed at small children. So ABC threw in the towel. You see, Etienne, you really were in league with the Devil—for don't you agree that the audio-visual world, with all its intricacies, its contacts, its endless delays, and its startling reversals, is the Devil incarnate?

● 1972. After the battles with "Tic et Tac, Toc et Poule," we had both grown fond of Christian Gallimard and Pierre Marchand, as well as Jean-Olivier Héron of the Gallimard publishing house. We shared our war stories, just like any other veterans. At the Bologna fair we all used to tend each other's exhibit booths, which gave rise to some

confusion among the competition. At the time you were dreaming of a new project aimed at young people: Trio, which would involve the publishers Gallimard and Bayard and yourself in audio-visuals. We all wanted the same thing, quality programs for children of all ages. Trio never achieved any legal status, but it still binds us together like an unwritten agreement.

▲ Whatever ups and downs life—or business—may have for us, we must remain true to our high standards of quality. The children's audience is no small thing. To the contrary. They demand further and greater effort, and even more honesty, for they cannot defend themselves, and everything we create for them has an impact on the rest of their lives.

■ 1974. A two-fold increase in the price of paper was killing off many publications with a large number of pages and low advertising revenues. Such was the case with Record, one of our monthly magazines for teenagers. In order not to lose the title's clout, we turned it into an oversized bi-monthly publication, completely in color and featuring the world's best illustrators. You agreed to act as art director, while Martin Berthommier assumed day-to-day responsibilities.

● I know few illustrators, graphic designers, or art directors in France who don't still cherish one or two precious issues of Record. Its audacity and visual quality were breathtaking. So much so that some readers and some parents never quite recovered. The new Record lasted for only two or three years, but it left an impression that is still lasting, indelible, and creative. Once again, you had left your mark.

▲ 1979. The Devil again reared his ugly head and

led you to a feature-length animated film, Supersaxo, with the subtitle (I'm not making this up) "Between God and the Devil." But, this marvelous film was never finished because one of its principal investors backed out. Five years at hard labor, five years during which you lost everything but your real friends. Lawyers and moneymen in four countries went crazy. It was a real and very enlightening vision of Hell. But you've done your penance now, and when you finally die, at least you'll only have to choose between Purgatory and Heaven.

■ 1980. Tired of seeing you always being tempted by the Devil, I decided to make a dramatic move and bring you into God's service. Okapi, our bimonthly for ten-to-fourteen-year-olds, planned a series of two-page spreads on Jesus. You were asked to illustrate it. The theme was simple and suited your nonconformist nature: Jesus' angry moments. On the left-hand page, the Gospel according to Pierre-Marie Beaude, on the right-hand page, according to Etienne Delessert. After dozens and dozens of pencil sketches on paper tablecloths in restaurants all over Paris and Lausanne, we finally had a book: Quinze Gestes de Jesus, made up of the pages that had appeared in the magazine. The fifteen drawings call for meditation and thought. I'm especially fond of "He Weeps," with that completely red face and white tear shaped like a skull. Death: the hyphen that joins God and the Devil, that links your two passions.

● 1991. Thirty years of work together. Thirty years of successes and failures on both sides. Thirty years of meetings, of restaurants, of long evenings, of experimentation, on railway-station platforms, in airport waiting rooms. For thirty years—despite the silences, the differences, the distances, whatever our separations, whatever our various plans and projects, whatever we may have been doing in the interim—we have always greeted each other again with that special look, a special gesture, as the brother neither of us ever had.

Yves Beccaria

1. Repetitive pattern for generations.

2. Families psychol. issues. Family tree - 2 people facing each other (alternate color - sexes)

3. Able to tell how rotten he feels (kind of satisfied to say it, in his deep hole)

4. Mother - father - child triangle - child is the looser

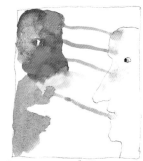

5. "taking back" projection emanating from the self

6. mental landscape, mental representation of people

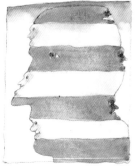

7) ambivalence good - bad within the self. (SEE OTHER SKETCH)

8) Emotionally absent (his self is flying away)

9) Anger, like nuclear waste, is non-degradable

I received a brochure at THE ATLANTIC MONTHLY in 1985. BACK IN THE USA, the cover announced. "Back?" He's been here *before*? Does Etienne Delessert actually *live* somewhere? Inside were not only wonderful pictures but also a note from him saying he would like to work with me. You must understand, this was like getting a résumé from Santa Claus applying for a summer job. This person I'd admired for years, who'd given me so much inspiration—I'd assumed he was some mythical creature. Or dead at the very least. Now I found he was not even very old—and BACK. With a phone call we began one of the most rewarding ongoing magazine collaborations I've ever been half of.

● In my college days, long before I'd discovered magazine art direction, when I thought the only way I could be deeply involved with both words and pictures was by writing and illustrating my own books, I had very few heroes. (I ask a lot of a hero.) Etienne was one of them. When my attempts at book illustration were called too sophisticated for children or too childlike for adults, Etienne's work presented a glimmer of hope for me. In his children's books, he had a way of getting into a child's mind, showing the seriousness of play. He seemed to understand how blurry the line is between childhood and adulthood, between curiosity and dread, between life and death. It's rare to find people who think the way you think. He seemed to, and it gave me courage at the time.

■ We've met only once, years after we'd begun working together. He looks quite like the characters he draws—no long, furry ears or anything peculiar like that, but a similar softness in his face and hands. He signed the first book of his I'd ever bought (some sixteen years earlier), probably with no idea how much it had meant to me.

▲ Most magazines that, like THE ATLANTIC, publish serious public-affairs articles don't pay much attention to their visual accompaniment. I, with my editor's blessing, have tried over the past ten years to enhance this sort of writing with meaningful and beautiful images from the best illustrators and fine artists without disturbing its sophisticated nature. My aim has been to make the information more accessible by appealing to another, more intuitive, part of the reader's brain.

● Who better than Etienne for this task? Although he has illustrated fiction, poetry, and light pieces for us, I depend on him most for those serious articles—usually the ones concerned with the mind or the heart. Often the subject is either children or one that evokes the child in us. He has applied his intelligent and elegant touch to themes ranging from patterns in love and marriage to the mental stability of therapists, from attachment theory and the raising of kids to the question of life on other planets.

■ This is how we work together: He's somewhere in the country in Connecticut and I'm in Boston. I call and describe the article. He, though generally swamped with work, agrees to take the assignment. (To my delight, not *once* has he turned us down.)

HE BECOMES SO INVOLVED WITH THE ARTICLE AND SURE OF HIS READING OF IT THAT I DO BELIEVE HE WOULD EDIT THE THING HIMSELF IF HE WERE ALLOWED TO.

As with all the people I commission art from, the story is sent. But, while I give many artists specific suggestions, directions to pursue, points to focus on, Etienne prefers to work with minimal guidance. He and I usually talk quite a lot about the article after he's read it, just to make sure we're on the same wavelength, and then he's off and running. I have never worked with an artist who became more intimately involved with the text than Etienne, and I wish I could explain what a joy this is. Many artists are frightened by words; they feel their personal expression may somehow be compromised by having to relate to the writer's ideas. Etienne is fearless. He seems to take delight in the challenge of translating those ideas into his own distinctive visual language. He is so serious about communicating things, so precise in his work. He seems always intellectually in control and yet he remains extremely playful in his interpretations, taking chances with other people's imaginations: such a surprising combination of care with seeming caprice.

▲ His little, color sketches arrive after a week or so, and when I open the package, it's like a Whitman's Sampler box of chocolates, all delicately labeled and luscious-looking. Since I've generally commissioned a series, the drawings, with his handwritten captions of quotes or specific points, are lined up in the order in which those points appear in the article, often all done on a single page.

● We then work out the details of size and shape. I might switch a cover idea for an inside one, pick my favorites, or suggest slight alterations. It is lucky that I and my editor are generally in agreement with Etienne's interpretations, because this artist is a stubborn man. He becomes so involved with the article and sure of his reading of it that I do believe he would edit the thing himself if he were allowed to. When the final art arrives, two weeks or so later, it is unusually similar to the sketches, just bigger and even more beautiful.

■ The first project we worked on together was a cover story by Bruno Bettelheim about the punishment and disciplining of children. That cover remains my favorite of all the things he's done for us, perhaps because it was the first—before I was used to his surprises. Rising out of a sunny landscape, behind a small, sweet-looking child, was a huge, dark-blue hand with eyes and a tooth-filled mouth. What amazed me was the immediate, visceral impact and clarity of meaning of what on closer scrutiny was quite an abstract concept. How does he communicate so directly with our psyches?

▲ I have a theory. Bear with me, it goes something like this: All your life, your feelings and thoughts are complex, but when you're little, your vocabulary is so minimal that any attempts to express them must be very simplistic. Some of your best concepts and fantasies you just give up on, some of your deepest fears you submerge or blank out, because there are no words to store them in. Grown people (many parents) often forget they ever had major anxieties, fresh ideas, or big thoughts as children, and then have trouble recognizing them and knowing what to do with them as adults. Perhaps it would be better if people were incapable of speech until they were, say, twenty-one and had decent vocabularies. If we weren't attempting to express things until we could do it right, do our

thoughts justice, they would flourish and emerge in their best state. But those early, heartfelt perceptions don't really disappear. They are expressed in children's dreams and nightmares. Though you may never put them into words, I think you remember those dream-pictures all your life.

● Luckily, Etienne Delessert not only remembers but has the extraordinary ability to draw them. In his colors, shadows, puddles, and clouds, his beasts, ghosts, and friendly faces, he both acknowledges the complexities of childhood and illuminates some of the simple truths of adulthood. I think that's his secret. And if you weren't fortunate enough as a child to have seen those pictures in Etienne's storybooks, you have a second chance now.

JUDY GARLAN

The reading experience of a critic specializing in children's literature is marked by a number of key books that stand out like beacons when one analyses one's work over the years, and those beacons reveal one's own personal view of what children's books are in the end to achieve. For me, along with Maurice Sendak's WHERE THE WILD THINGS ARE and André Hodeir and Tomi Ungerer's WARWICK'S 3 BOTTLES, THE ENDLESS PARTY and Eugène Ionesco's STORY NUMBER 1 and STORY NUMBER 2 illustrated by Etienne Delessert have, since their first appearance, been among the most important landmarks in establishing the legitimacy of the illustrator's full participation in the creation of children's books, a legitimacy that I was determined to promote, but one that in those days few were willing to acknowledge.

■ Upon the first publication of THE ENDLESS PARTY by Editions Quist-Vidal in 1967 in France, Delessert's originality and inventive imaginative power were at once recognized, but the book also gave rise to critical controversy among teachers and librarians. It was at once avant-garde and an instant classic of artistic illustration. In making the Biblical adventures of the patriarch Noah and his animals in the Ark during the Flood accessible to late-twentieth-century children, with text and images that formed a cohesive whole, Delessert was already unequivocally putting into practice his concept of children's book illustration: "By brushing against the surface of reality I bring into existence a parallel world that is like a rubbing of the real one from which it derives its strength... Its exaggeratedly animist and childlike elements help to make it a part of the cosmic picture children rely on to explain phenomena in their own way."

▲ It is obvious that the artist enjoys telling stories, enjoys embodying an entire symbolic structure in an image, attempting to express in his illustrations "with apparent logic all the illogicality of the subconscious." Delessert became Eugène Ionesco's collaborator and illustrator in STORY NUMBER 1 and 2, participating in word games in which everyone seems to speak nonsense until their words become part of the Great Game of Total Poetry. The illustrator, in a playful spiral of absurdity, gives the words colors, turns them into images of objects and flowers. Thus, Delessert single-handedly invented the game of co-reading, wherein the aesthetic reality of the work, discovered in an atmosphere of affective intimacy between parent and child, suddenly acquires an entirely new sociocultural dimension.

● There can be no question that from then on each children's book by Etienne Delessert has been hailed as an artistic event. Such was certainly the case with HOW THE MOUSE WAS HIT ON THE HEAD BY A STONE AND SO DISCOVERED THE WORLD. In 1971, he worked with Professor Jean Piaget and the children of a Lausanne school to set forth coherent replies to the basic questions about the world put to him by his young readers. The book's

EVERYTHING IS THERE FOR A REASON, DEMANDING THAT THE READER ABSORB ALL THE SHADES OF THE WORDS AND DWELL ON EVERY IMAGE. EVERYTHING HAS A MEANING, EVERYTHING IS A SIGN.

concept is specifically childlike, as is the strong visual impact of its graphics and Delessert's vivid colors.

■ Whether illustrating Rudyard Kipling's JUST SO STORIES, Gordon Lightfoot's THE PONY MAN, Madame d'Aulnoy's BEAUTY AND THE BEAST, or Michel Déon's THOMAS ET L'INFINI, or summoning from his palette the seven brilliant spots of color and three expensive lines that form the elf named Yok-Yok (who by his provocative questions helps every child marvel at creation and confront life and ever-present death) Delessert has been a creator of characters and an animator-director fully aware of the importance of environment and setting in giving a story all its cosmic dimensions.

▲ The human universe is inconceivable to him without the presence of animals, whether familiar or exotic. The themes of the mythical tales that haunt Delessert demand an iconography in which nature is always present, a symbolic representation that will be both immediately perceptible to today's young reader and eternal in its imagery.

● Delessert, who learned from Piaget that literature can modify a child's vision of the world so long as it is poetic and allows room for the imagination, has continued to create books for co-reading. Aimed at adults as well as children, his images, even those for the very young, invite myriad interpretations, a hundred whys and becauses.

■ In A LONG LONG SONG, based on the popular nursery rhyme, Delessert carried to the furthest limits the ambiguity of word and image and the interactions between them. The questions posed during this stroll through the woods and fields in the company of Father Winter are linked not so much to the visual logic of the song's correlative parallelism as they are to what is implicit and unspoken in the atmosphere that the landscape painter creates for us.

▲ In ASHES, ASHES, Delessert meditates on the flow of life, on past, present, and future. The English title may be more enlightening than the French LA CORNE DE BRUME, or "The Foghorn," for it reveals the inspiration for the painter-poet's daydreams. From the very first image on the book's jacket, the reader realizes this will be an initiatory voyage. On the prow of the canoe in which the hero sets forth the yin-yang diagram is drawn, like an echo. Against the setting sun, paddle in hand, a figure—half-man, half-hare—propels his bark across the calm waters of the lake. Near him in the boat are a violin and a backpack, out of which a goose-feather pen is sticking and on which Yok-Yok is perched. Everything is there for a reason, demanding that the reader absorb all the shades of the words and dwell on every image. Everything has a meaning, everything is a sign.

● The three visitors who await the hero on the threshold of his house can, with Christian symbolism, stand for the three functions of the child Jesus: king, priest, and prophet. Or perhaps they are the beggar, cripple, and corpse that led the Buddha to meditate on the world's reality and to conclude that each man's life amounts to a bowl of ashes. "Ashes, ashes…" all Delessert's ambiguity is contained in the words. In whatever way we read it, the encounter with the visitor leads to metamorphosis and questioning.

■ The landscapes become mythical and the narrative is constantly metaphorical. The hero of this

fable, speaking in the first person, sorts through his memories, his deeds, and his friendships, and attempts to protect himself from the magic spells around him. Some day he will discover what is essential. Then—"I reached the first patches of snow and could barely hear the horn any more. So I played my own song loud."—he will finally see the mist rise and, reaching the shore of the lake, be rewarded by a woman's soft smile.

▲ The images, with their plastic beauty, haloed by a magical and luminescent glow, are very moving. The words seem to whisper in our ears. We can open the pages of this book over and over and each time we will find a different message, according to the hour of day and the mood of our reading, and depending upon whether we listen more intently to the song of the foghorn or the song of the violin.

● And yet, whatever its meanderings, the poet's voyage becomes the reader's, adult or child. Dedicated to his son Adrien, who is still a little boy, this personal tale—as is always the case with Delessert's work—has nevertheless been made universal: a message to every child of this millennium's last generation.

JANINE DESPINETTE

But if your hero happens to be both alive and also a practicing artist, you're taking a real chance. For instance, what happens if everything he produces after a certain point disappoints? Deposing a true hero can be traumatic. But, on the other hand, suppose your living, practicing artist hero gets better over time. Not only does your faith in him grow, but so does your self-confidence. After all, you selected him in the first place. Etienne Delessert has been a hero of mine for over twenty years and has given no indication of abdication or grounds for demotion. He was unknowingly elevated to my personal Olympus while I was still a student. If choosing a living, practicing artist for a hero is dangerous, making that choice as an eager, impressionable art student is downright reckless.

● There I was studying architecture at the Rhode Island School of Design when I had the remarkable good fortune of learning to draw with one Thomas Sgouros, another permanent resident of the aforementioned mount. Professor Sgouros introduced me to the pleasures and possibilities of seeing, particularly as applied to the creation and appreciation of pictures. A new world opened up into which I leapt with youthful exuberance and a ravenous appetite. Among the many things I saw, as if for the first time, were picture books, and one of the two or three I can still remember as if it were yesterday is Delessert's THE ENDLESS PARTY. To these wide eyes, every element of each illustration seemed to be in exactly the right place, each complete unto itself yet simultaneously contributing to the success of the whole.

SPACE REMAINS PRIMARILY AN INTELLECTUAL CONCEPT, IMPLIED BY OVERLAPPING FORMS, SIMPLE CHANGES IN SIZE AND THE OCCASIONAL REFERENCE TO PERSPECTIVE, RATHER THAN THE DIMINUTION OF CLARITY OR COLOR INTENSITY WE ARE ACCUSTOMED TO IN REAL LIFE.

■ Perhaps I can best explain, and in the process perhaps justify, both my initial and continued admiration for Delessert's work with the following example. There is an illustration in THE ENDLESS PARTY which for me comes as close to perfection as possible. In the top third of the page, a parrot leans down from its perch and squawks most threateningly at a mischievous monkey, who occupies the lower two thirds. The monkey has just extracted a fistful of feathers from the tail of the understandably savage Psittaciforme. The subsequent confrontation between parrot and monkey is initially underscored by their separateness. The animals never touch. In fact both are completely surrounded and kept apart by clean white space. They even have their own themes: The parrot's is rage, the monkey's play. But the page is far from static. The appearance of isolation and containment is wonderfully deceptive. The feathers and beak of the parrot and the arms and legs of the monkey are brilliantly arranged so as to encourage the eye to ride a pinwheel of shape and color as it spins wildly around the monkey's open self-protecting hand. Yet, the chase or counterattack is only implied. The real fireworks take place in our imaginations, which are fueled by the subject matter and ignited by the way in which its arrangement leads our eyes. The illustration is a feast of playful contradiction, masterfully achieving motion and chaos by offering stability and order.

▲ The parrot and monkey, along with all the other animals in the book, are primarily creations of Delessert's extraordinary imagination. Each is a dazzling mosaic of shapes, colors, patterns, and texture, so skillfully designed and subtly modeled as to appear full of personality and life. They are far more believable and compelling than more literal images of the same animals could ever hope to be.

● But it's been twenty-three years since this Noah and his artful ark intoxicated me with the pleasures of pictorial perfection. Their creator is very much alive and producing and, of course, continually putting his hero status on the line. Not to worry, Etienne. In his two most recent books, A Long Long Song and Ashes, Ashes, we are transported across snow and water, by boat and cloud, into the middle of Delessert's own imagined world. To be sure, there are familiar clues which allow us initial access. We recognize bits of New England architecture, lawns and trees, streets and vistas. Stylized yet unmistakably human forms lure us into each magical tale, each mysterious journey. But no sooner do we feel at home in this world than its creator populates it with a host of extraordinary creatures, fashioned from a combination of recognizable shapes such as a pig's snout or a rabbit's ears, and an army of fantastic symbols. Not surprisingly, these creatures are both strange and strangely endearing, more so in fact than any of the human protagonists that lead us into the stories in the first place.

■ While both texts are full of intentional ambiguity, and in the case of Ashes, Ashes increasingly evocative imagery, what makes both books so compelling is their visual supremacy. Once again we must believe what we see and yet we are never allowed to take it for granted. Both are more ambitious and more personal than The Endless Party (time has a tendency to do that in the right hands) and the art, not surprisingly, is more sophisticated. One need only compare the owl in The Endless Party with the owl in A Long Long Song. Both are complete and beautifully designed, yet the latter, while no less a product of Delessert's imagination, is the beneficiary of twenty-odd years of continuous practice.

▲ Even if I don't understand every word the first or even the fifth time I read these books, I am repeatedly struck by Delessert's extraordinary ability to weave together confusion and order, the bizarre and the familiar, the grotesque and the charming into a highly personal yet universally accessible world. As in The Endless Party, flatness prevails, underscoring the fact that whether ultimately painted or left untouched, pristine, every square centimeter of each image has been lovingly considered. Even in the later books, with their more realistic landscapes, space remains primarily an intellectual concept implied by overlapping forms, simple changes in size, and the occasional reference to perspective, rather than the diminution of clarity or color intensity we are accustomed to in real life. Everything remains in focus no matter how far away we believe it to be.

● As he has in the past, in all of his books and all of his pictures, Etienne Delessert will continue to take us on the journey he wishes us to experience. The trees may change shape and the surfaces may become even richer, but each new journey will arise from images of precision and surprise, intellect and affection. My hero.

DAVID MACAULAY

ASHES, ASHES WATERCOLOR 1990

It is, however, just one doorway through which to enter his world, without any special explanation of it or any explicit definition given to it. There is a quiet, tree-lined street with small buildings (one is a post office) and two American flags; there is gray pavement and tidy flower beds all the same size; there are the long shadows of a bright and ominously silent afternoon. In this drawing, Delessert's particular melancholy appears in the same ways

ONE IS IMMEDIATELY TAKEN BY THE HORRIFIC CHARMS OF HIS DEBONAIR MONSTERS; WHILE PAUSING TO SAVOR THE COUNTLESS EMBELLISHMENTS HE PROVIDES, WE ARE GRIPPED BY THE UNPARALLELED WICKEDNESS OF HIS ALCHEMICAL MIXTURES.

and with the same symbols as Jean Piaget spoke of in reference to HOW THE MOUSE WAS HIT ON THE HEAD BY A STONE AND SO DISCOVERED THE WORLD, in 1970. In that entrancing and elusive book, Delessert was acting as a demiurge. While telling how a mouse discovered and got to know the world, he was actually defining his own world, a universe made up of ambiguous pleasures, of serenities hanging on the brink of nightmares, of dreams artfully made indecipherable.

▲ Fairy tales, we know, are but collective dreams. Delessert's illustrations of the famous fairy tale BEAUTY AND THE BEAST, in 1984, reinforce this definition. After all, in dreams just as in fairy tales, reality and fiction mingle, and, in this respect, Delessert is ever an illustrator of fairy tales. The drawings of BEAUTY AND THE BEAST renovate the ancient mixtures of elements familiar to the Italian painters and designers who represented and defined the pagan soul of the Renaissance. Surfaces are delicate, melting away in the limpid brush strokes of watercolor; then comes the pen, to finish, out-

line, and distort with the implacable levity of an ancient scribe.

■ The proper setting of this book is, to an extent, the small Italian town of Bomarzo, with its garden of monsters, which expresses the eternal ambiguity of beauty and monstrosity. We are at Bomarzo, but also in front of a cathedral, better still in front of the cathedral of Notre-Dame, because in the universe of dreams and fairy tales, which his pictures come from, Delessert is forever a citizen of the same world in which Victor Hugo placed his monsters. Hugo's watercolors, the bold ink stains, the violent and knowing streaks, make up one of the great visual encyclopedias of the western fairy tale tradition.

● In the street with its flags and post office, in the afternoon silence of a day like any other, we look at the world through the eyes of an astonished mouse, but above all we wait for something which is about to happen. Archimboldo's universe starts to be defined here, in a place where no Beast or monsters are in sight, but where all is ready because they are coming.

▲ A world studied, understood, and narrated by a mouse that has been consulting Jean Piaget (indeed, appearing in the same drawing with the great psychologist) is a world seen through eyes very capable of searching and inventing. The mouse's world is the world of Archimboldo and Hoffmann, a world strewn with the moody inventions of Nodier's romantic malice. Above all, it is the world of the PUER AETERNUS. The secret protagonist of Delessert's visual world is, indeed, the PUER AETERNUS, the disquieting child deity strangely smiling at livid dawns and silent sunsets. In the afternoon, when a perfectly honest tree-lined street turns into something ominous, just as in those dawns and sunsets, the PUER AETERNUS suggests a new mode of perception.

■ There are very complex reminiscences, such as those in the first drawing of ASHES, ASHES, in 1990, of a canoe sailing on a remote lake in a silence so absolute that it can be painted. The memories refer back to the bleak paintings of the traveling painters of the nineteenth century and, even more so, to the dreams those paintings elicited in countless children. In a universe so uncertain as to its arrangement, nature, and culture mingle. In the pictures in ASHES, ASHES there are rocks so real, so massive and detailed, as to remind us of a geologist keen on presenting every nuance in a truly scientific fashion. And then, in one of the heartbreaking, doleful drawings in FLOWERS FOR ALGERNON, from 1988, the main character is reading Sartre's memoirs; it might happen that he runs into the child Sartre swimming in the words of the LAROUSSE, enraptured by his immersion in the dictionary.

● A geologist's precision in describing the rocks and at the same time the accuracy of bibliographic details within the epiphany of sorrow, which makes Algernon the secret protagonist of many anxieties in our world: how can one be an illustrator in this way and yet preserve the mocking teratological irony which is sprinkled throughout and points to a knowing association with Hieronymous Bosch? Perhaps because great illustrators, unlike painters, know they must live and work at the convergence of complex worlds, forever synthesizing others' fictions and universes with their own to bring them to life. Delessert converses with the entire visual heritage of the western world, paying homage to Callot, laughing over Piranesi's darkness, constructing his drawings with the same provocative complexity as a Biedermeier craftsman.

▲ The big gray cats watching City Hall in a picture from A LONG LONG SONG, from 1988, are about to break into the demonic saraband, thus turning sly composure into an almost infernal dance. As in some old Italian popular prints, in Delessert's drawings too, Carnival passes quickly to Lent, and a composed, devout procession turns into a TOTENTANZ. In Delessert's pictures, the rhetorical figure of the oxymoron scores its conceptual victory. While yielding to his elegant sweetness, one is immediately taken by the horrific charms of his debonair monsters; while pausing to savor the countless embellishments he provides, we are gripped by the unparalleled wickedness of his alchemical mixtures.

■ Someone once wrote that style is the devil's work. In his particular hell, Delessert would indeed be able to exorcise the demons, attacking them with the wondrous flexibility of his drawing, the funambulist's elegance of his stroke, and the knowingness of his cultural references.

ANTONIO FAETI

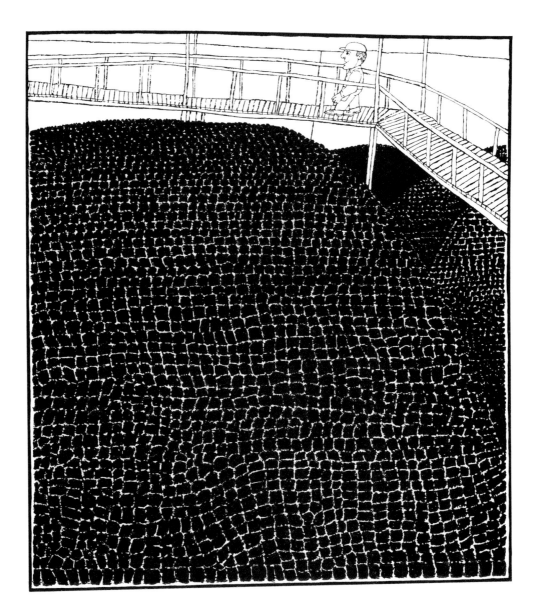

SHELL EMULAX GOUACHE 1965

JOHN K. GALBRAITH FORTUNE MAGAZINE INK 1967

STORY NUMBER 1 GOUACHE 1968

· 32 ·

LE MATCH VALAIS-JUDÉE PENCIL 1968

· 34 ·

LE MATCH VALAIS-JUDÉE PENCIL 1968

HOW THE MOUSE... ACRYLIC 1971

· 39 ·

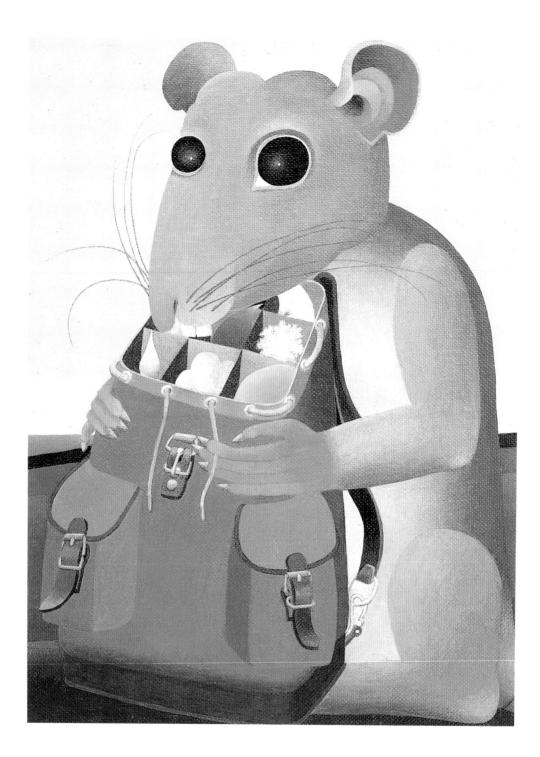

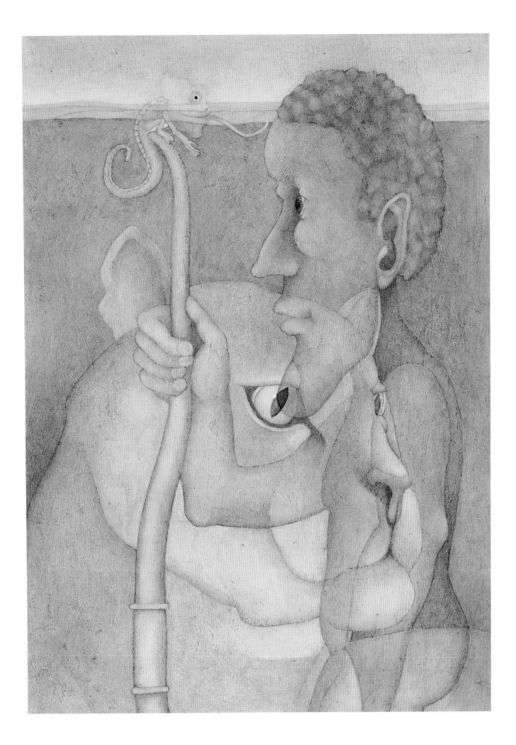

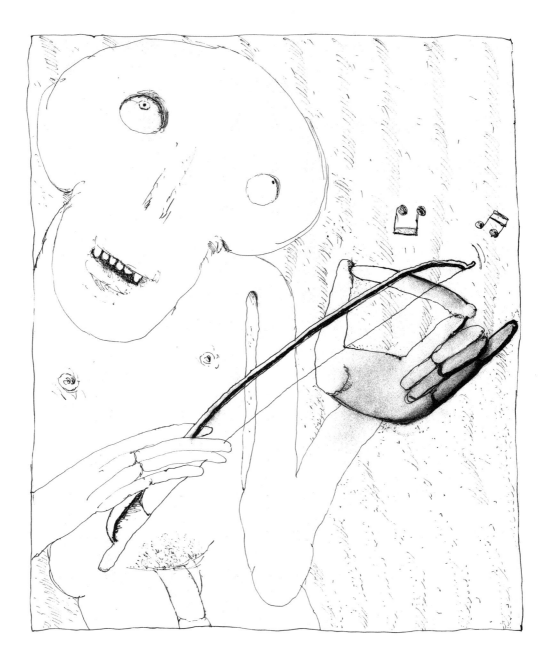

DANCE OF DEATH ACRYLIGRAPHY 1976

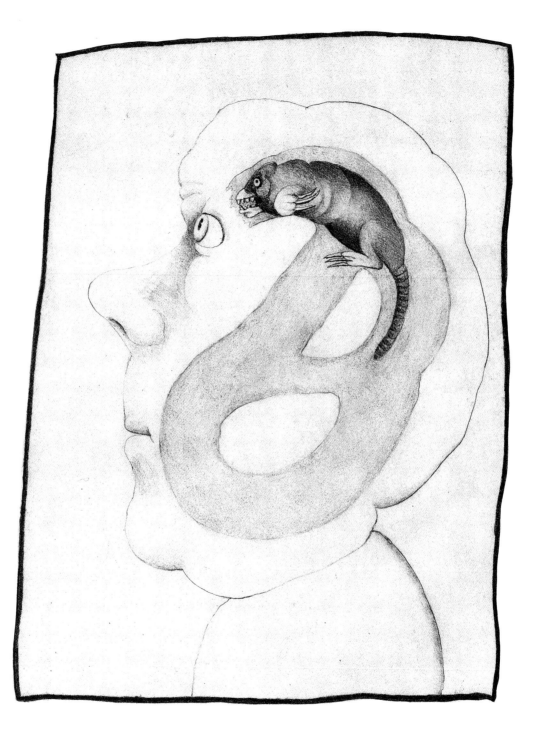

DANCE OF DEATH ACRYLIGRAPHY 1976

DANCE OF DEATH PENCIL 1973–74

DANCE OF DEATH WATERCOLOR 1974

THOMAS ET L'INFINI WATERCOLOR 1975

THOMAS ET L'INFINI WATERCOLOR 1975

THOMAS ET L'INFINI WATERCOLOR 1975

FIRE WATERCOLOR 1975

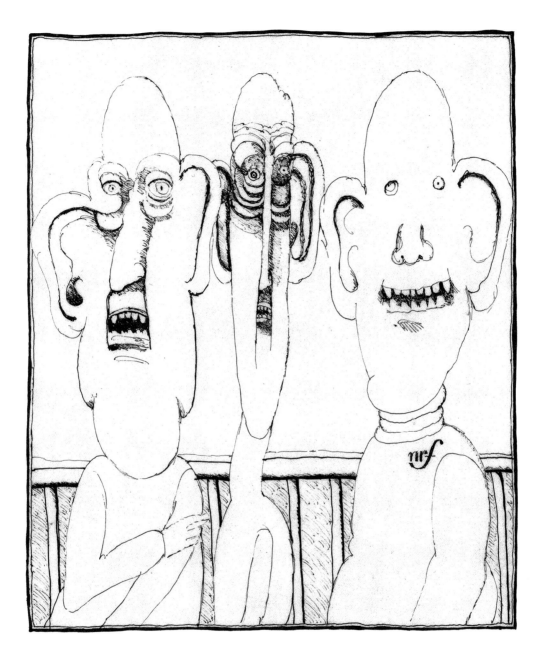

GALLIMARD, THREE GENERATIONS ACRYLIGRAPHY 1976

LE ROMAN DE RENART CHARCOAL 1977

· 64 ·

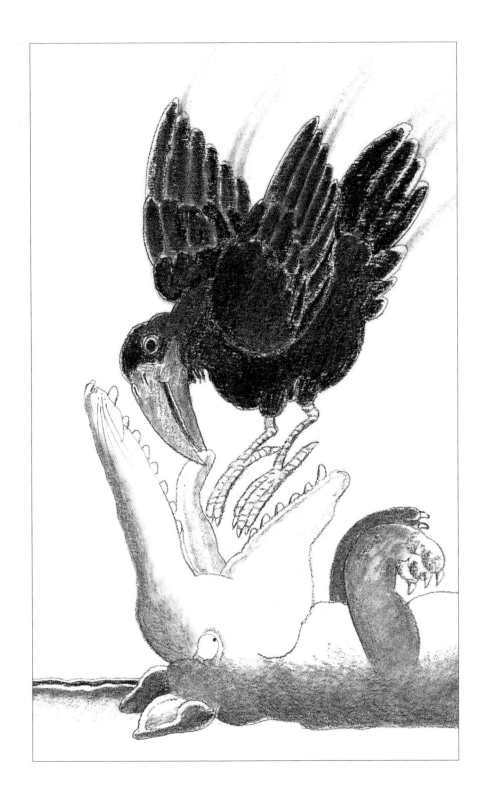

THE SEVEN FAMILIES OF LAKE PIPPLE-POPPLE WATERCOLOR 1978

· 69 ·

YOK-YOK ANIMATED FILM INK 1978

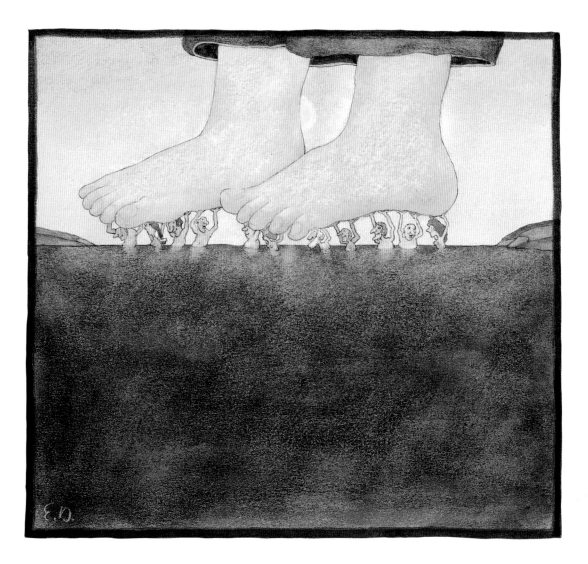

PETIT CROQUE WATERCOLOR 1982

· 85 ·

L'Âne Blanc ink and watercolor 1982

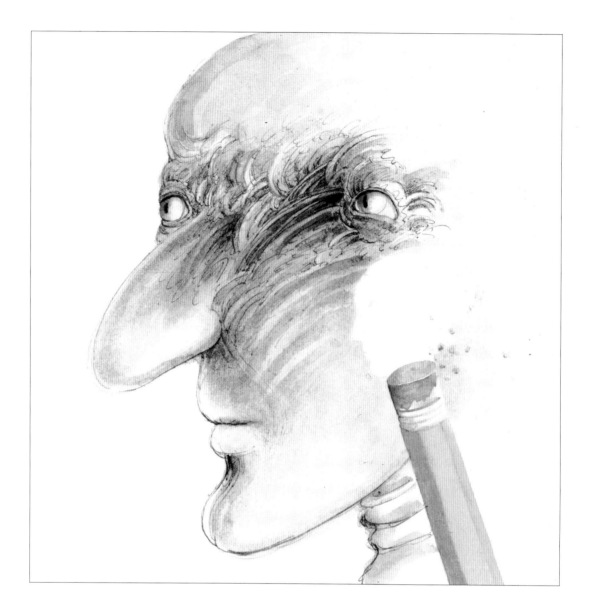

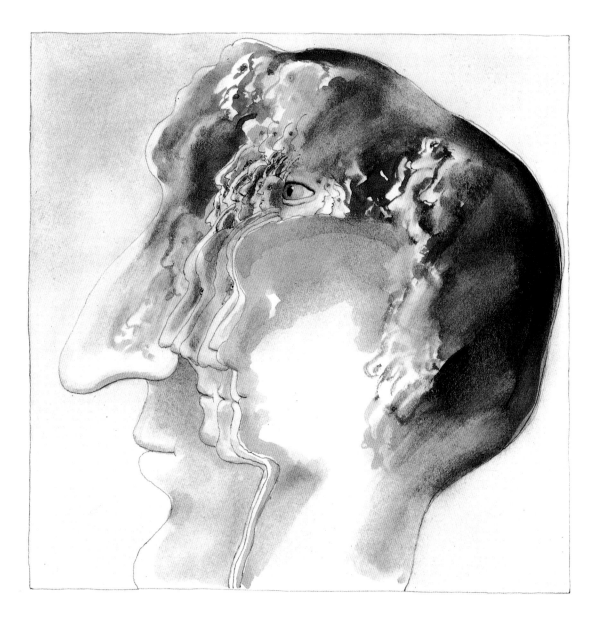

NOTRE AMI LE TEMPS INK AND WATERCOLOR 1982

· 89 ·

A Christmas Memory pencil 1984

LES TRÉSORS DE NOTRE ENFANCE 1   WATERCOLOR   1985

RITA WATERCOLOR 1985

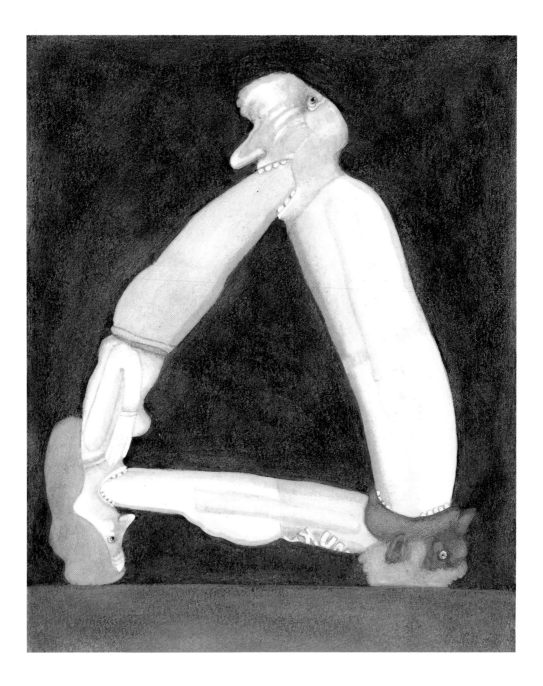

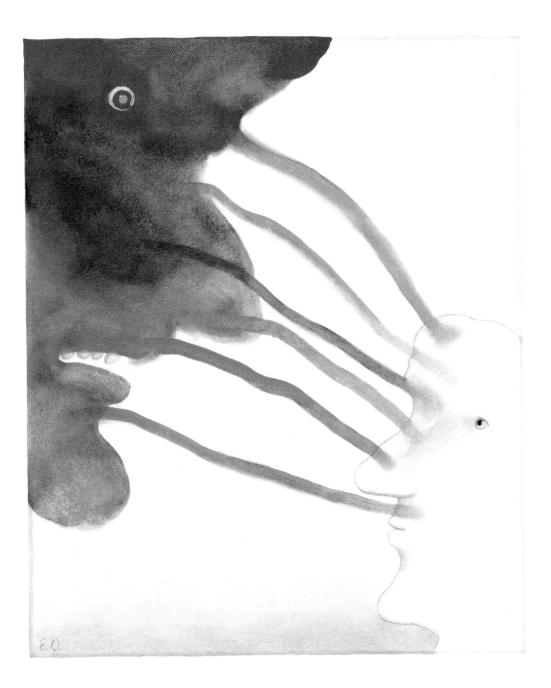

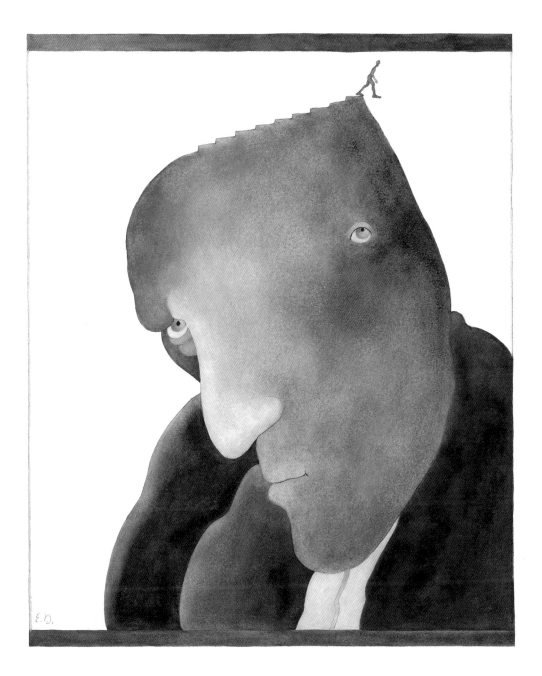

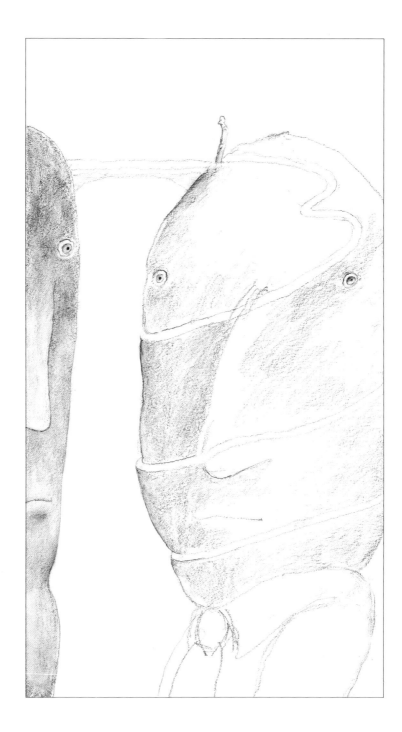

THE ANGEL OF THE BRIDGE   PENCIL   1987

· 112 ·

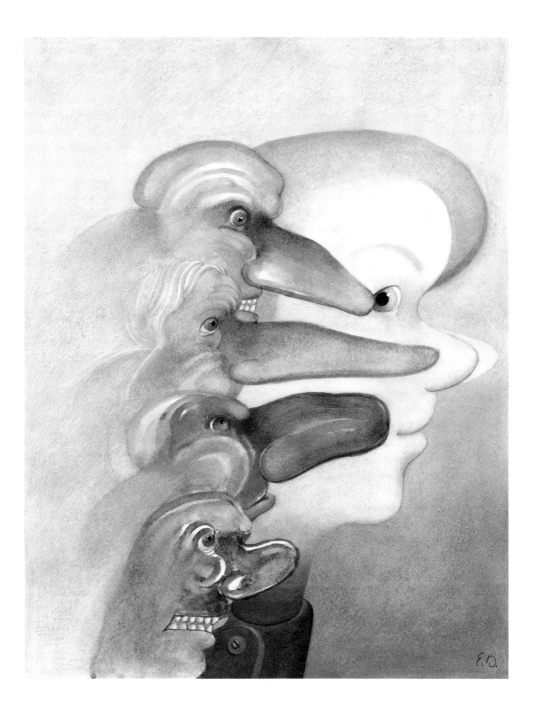

PINOCCHIO THEATER POSTER WATERCOLOR 1987

· 117 ·

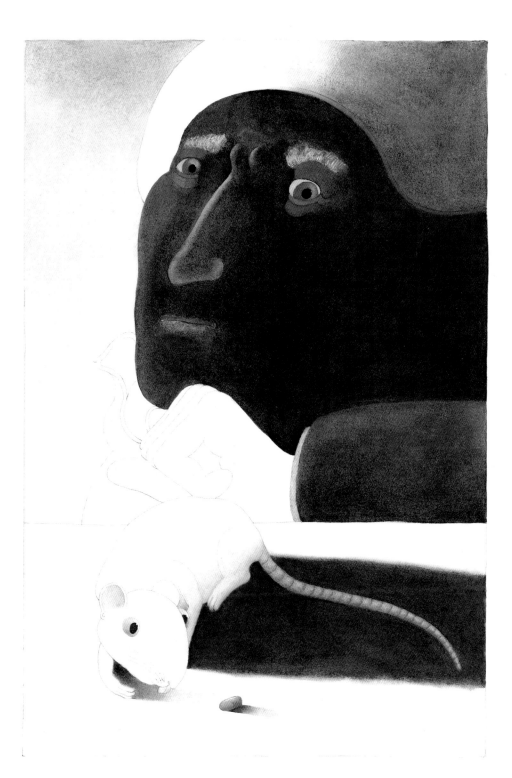

FLOWERS FOR ALGERNON WATERCOLOR 1988

A Long Long Song watercolor 1988

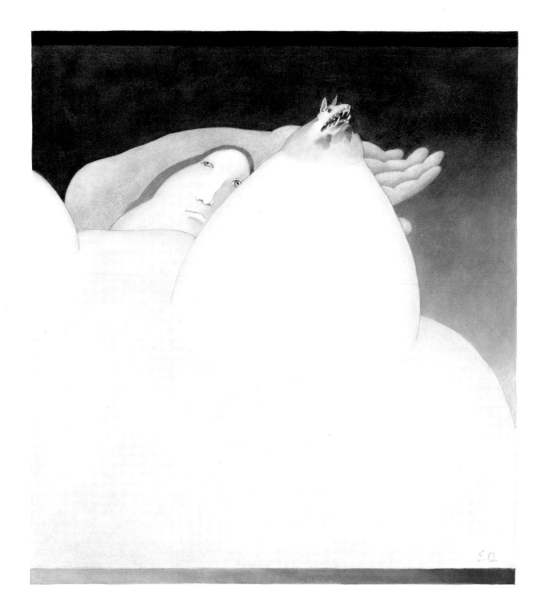

· 128 ·

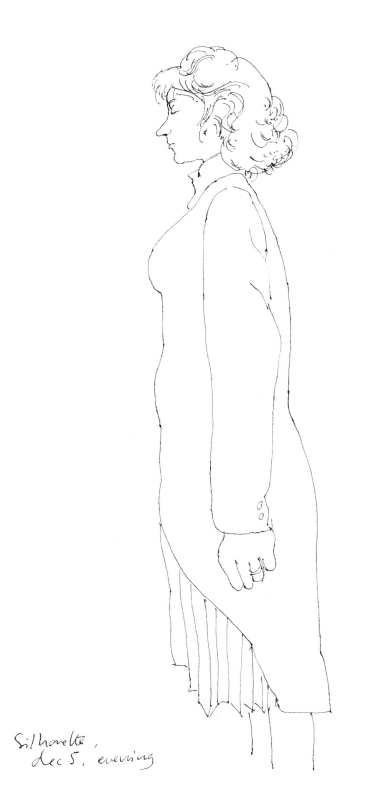

Silhouette,
dec 5, evening

RITA, EXPECTING INK 1987

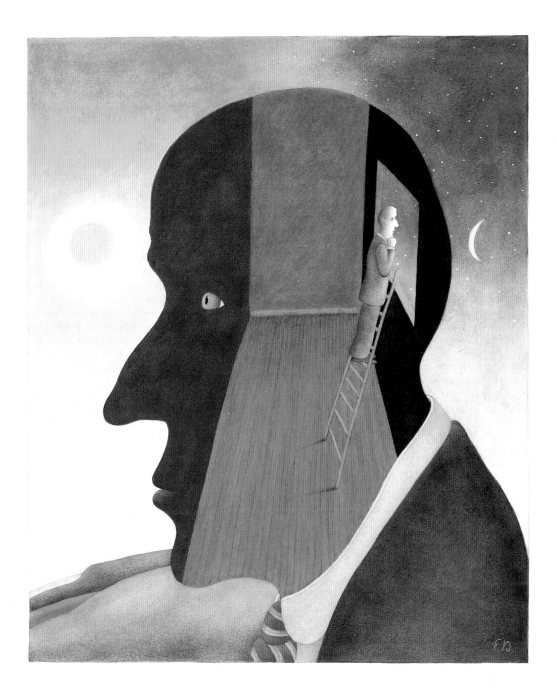

SEVILLA EXPO '92 POSTER WATERCOLOR 1989

· 135 ·

ASHES, ASHES WATERCOLOR 1990

ASHES, ASHES WATERCOLOR 1990

ASHES, ASHES WATERCOLOR 1990

ASHES, ASHES WATERCOLOR 1990

LES TRÉSORS DE NOTRE ENFANCE 2 WATERCOLOR 1990

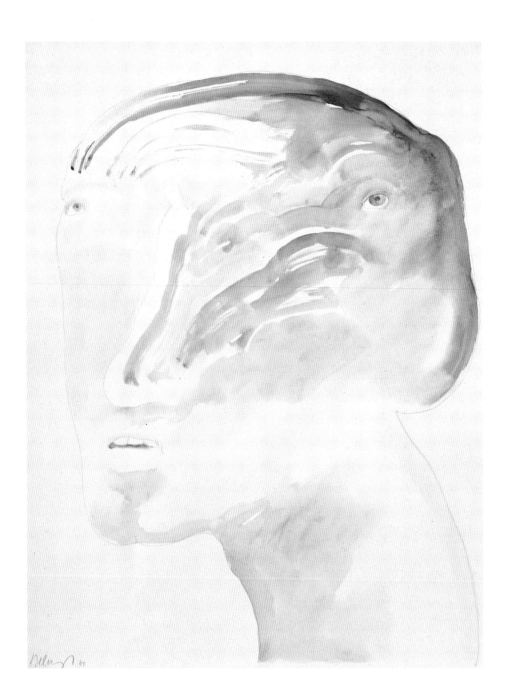

PROPHETS AND PRETENDERS, BRAIDED TONGUE   ACRYLIC   1980

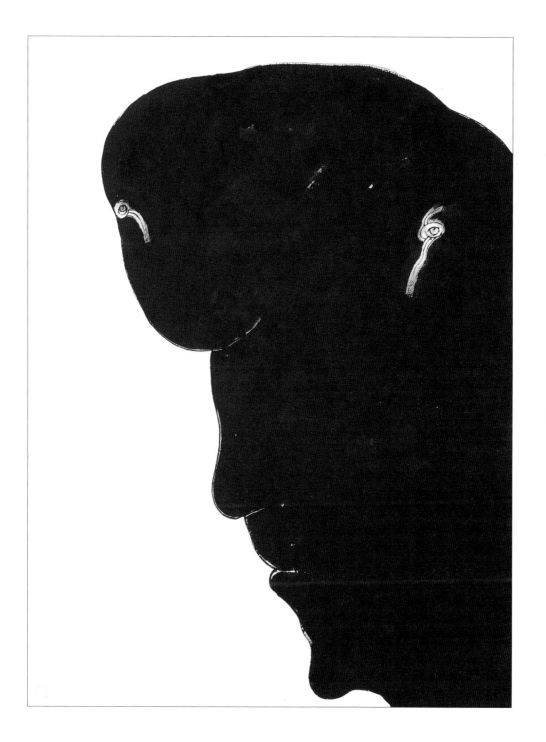

PROPHETS AND PRETENDERS INK 1985

· 147 ·

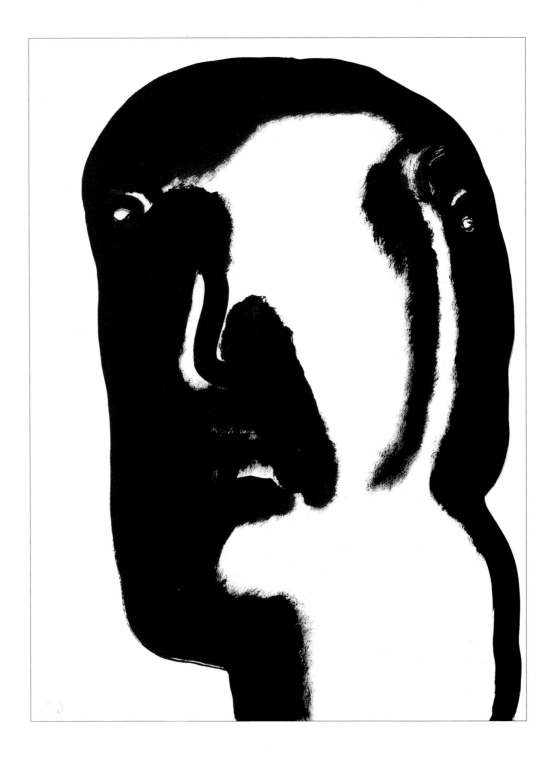

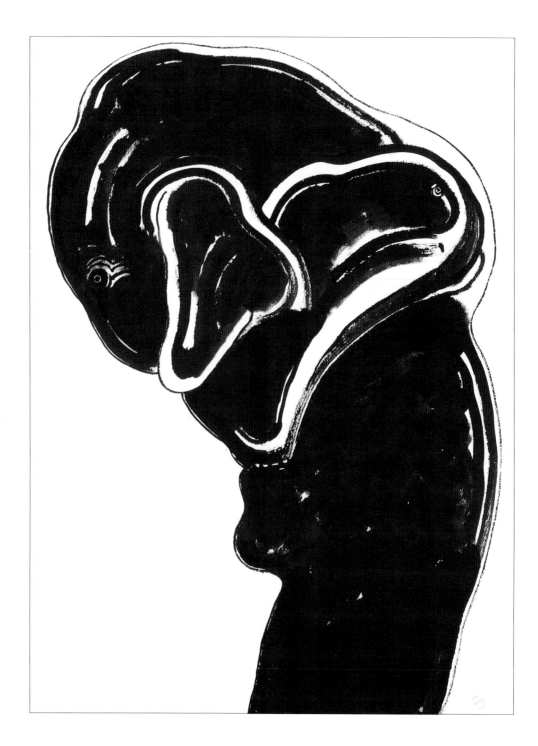

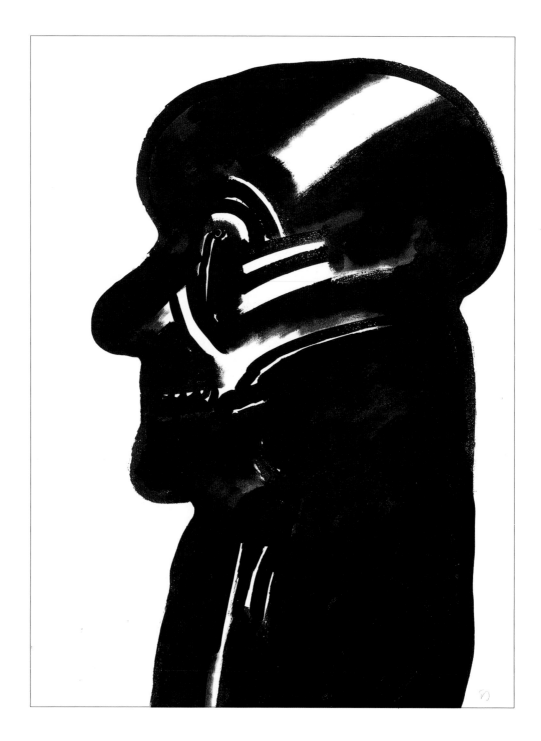

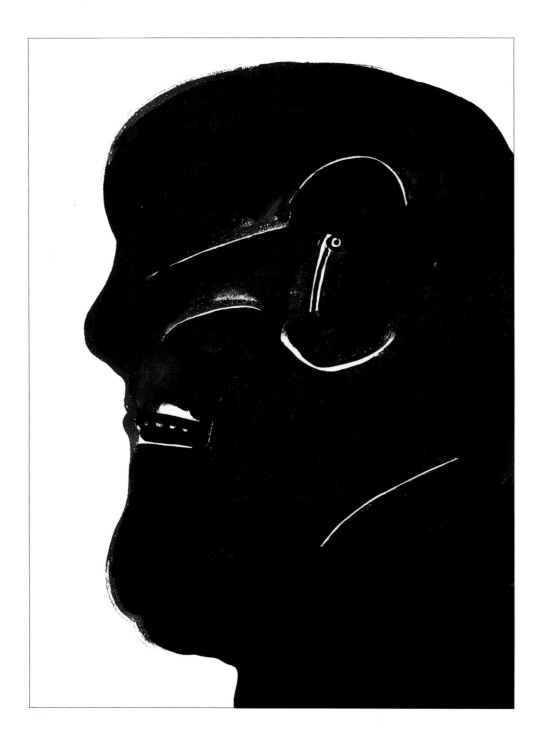

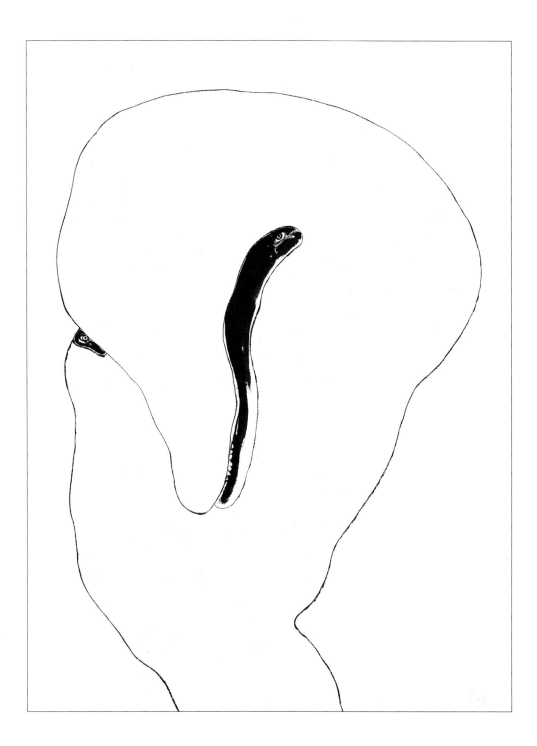

PROPHETS AND PRETENDERS INK 1990

· 154 ·

PROPHETS AND PRETENDERS OIL 1991

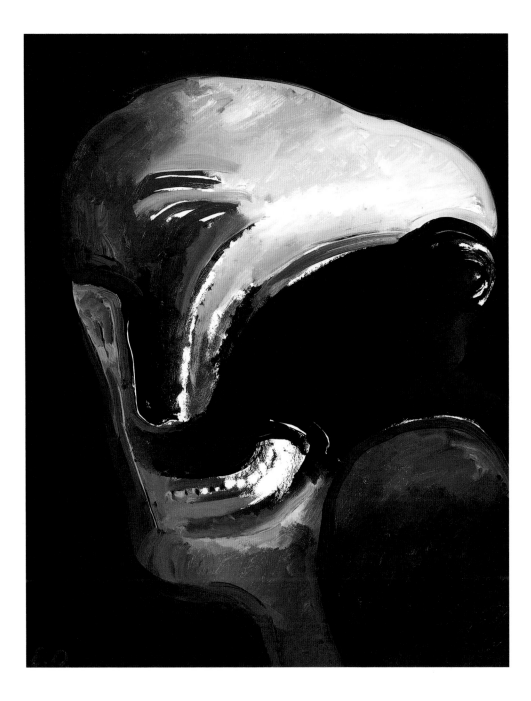

Books written and illustrated by Etienne Delessert

THE ENDLESS PARTY, written with Eleonore Schmid. New York: Harlin Quist, 1967. Re-issued in 1980 by Oxford University Press, Oxford. In Dan., Eng., Fr., and Ger.

HOW THE MOUSE WAS HIT ON THE HEAD BY A STONE AND SO DISCOVERED THE WORLD, with a foreword by Jean Piaget. New York: Good Book-Doubleday, 1971. In Eng., Fr., Ger., Gr., It., and Sp.

HAPPY BIRTHDAYS, with Rita Marshall. New York: Stewart, Tabori & Chang, 1986. In Eng.

A LONG LONG SONG. New York: Farrar, Straus and Giroux-Michael di Capua Books, 1988. In Eng , Fr., and Sp.

ASHES, ASHES. New York: Stewart, Tabori & Chang, 1990. In Eng. and Fr.

Books illustrated by Etienne Delessert

KAFKA CONTRE L'ABSURDE, by Joël Jakubec. Lausanne: Cahiers de la Renaissance Vaudoise, 1962. In Fr.

STORY NUMBER 1 FOR CHILDREN UNDER THREE YEARS OF AGE, by Eugène Ionesco. New York: Harlin Quist, 1968. In Dan., Dut., Eng., Fr., Ger., It., and Jap.

THE SECRET SELLER, by Betty Jean Lifton. New York: W.W. Norton, 1968. In Eng.

A WART SNAKE IN A FIG TREE, by George Mendoza. New York: Dial Press, 1968. In Eng.

LE MATCH VALAIS-JUDÉE, by Maurice Chappaz. Lausanne: Cahiers de la Renaissance Vaudoise, 1968. In Fr. and Ger.

STORY NUMBER 2 FOR CHILDREN UNDER THREE YEARS OF AGE, by Eugène Ionesco. New York: Harlin Quist, 1970. In Dan., Dut., Eng., Fr., Ger., and Jap.

LA CONFESSION DU PASTEUR BURG, by Jacques Chessex. Lausanne: Le Livre du Mois, 1970. In Fr.

JUST SO STORIES, by Rudyard Kipling. New York: Doubleday, 1972. In Eng., Fr., and Ger.

THE PONY MAN, by Gordon Lightfoot. New York: Harper's Magazine Press, 1972. In Eng. and Fr.

BEING GREEN, by Joseph G. Raposo. New York: Children's Television Workshop and Western Publishing, 1973. In Eng. and Fr.

THOMAS ET L'INFINI, by Michel Déon. Paris: Gallimard, 1975. In Fr. and Jap.

DIE MAUS UND DIE SCHMETTERLINGE, DIE MAUS UND DIE GIFTCHEN, and DIE MAUS UND DER LÄRM, by Anne van der Essen. Köln: Middelhauve, 1975. In Dut., Fr., Ger., Gr., It., and Jap.

LE ROMAN DE RENART. Paris: Gallimard, 1977. In Fr.

THE HAPPY PRINCE, by Oscar Wilde. Paris: Gallimard, 1977. In Fr.

THE GOLD BUG, by Edgar Allan Poe. Paris: Gallimard, 1977. In Fr.

DIE MAUS UND WAS IHR BLEIBT, by Anne van der Essen. Köln: Middelhauve, 1977. In Dut., Eng., Fr., Ger., Gr., It., and Jap. under the title AMELIA THE MOUSE AND HER GREAT-GREAT-GRANDCHILD.

LA SOURIS S'EN VA-T'EN GUERRE, by Anne van der Essen. Paris: Gallimard, 1978. In Fr.

THE SEVEN FAMILIES OF LAKE PIPPLE-POPPLE, by Edward Lear. Paris: Gallimard, 1978. In Fr.

PAROLES, by Jacques Prévert. Paris: Gallimard-Rombaldi, 1979. In Fr.

THE EARTH, THE WATER, THE AIR, and THE WORM, by Andrienne Soutter-Perrot. Lausanne: Tournesol, 1979. In Dan., Dut., Eng., Fr., Ger., Gr., It., Port., and Sp.

YOK-YOK, by Anne van der Essen; THE BLACKBIRD, THE FROG, THE WIZARD, THE NIGHT, THE RABBIT, and THE CATERPILLAR. Lausanne: Tournesol, 1979. In Eng., Fr., Ger., Gr., Heb., It., Per., Port., and Sp.

YOK-YOK, by Anne van der Essen; L'OMBRE, LE CIRQUE, LE GRILLON, LA NEIGE, LE VIOLON, and LA CERISE. Lausanne: Tournesol, 1980. In Fr., Ger., Gr., Heb., It., Per., Port., and Sp.

LE GRAND LIVRE DE YOK-YOK, by Anne van der Essen. Lausanne: Tournesol, 1981. In Fr.

QUINZE GESTES DE JÉSUS, by Pierre-Marie Beaude & Jean Debruynne. Paris: Okapi-Centurion Jeunesse, 1981. In Fr. and Ger.

L'Amour-Petit Croque et Ses Amis, by Christophe Gallaz, François Baudier and Jean Touvet. Lausanne: Tournesol, 1982. In Fr.

Le Temps, by François Nourissier. Denges, (Swi.): Au Verseau, 1982. In Fr.

Des Cinq Sens, by Jacques Chessex. Denges, (Swi.): Au Verseau, 1983. In Fr.

A Christmas Memory, by Truman Capote. Mankato: Creative Education, 1984. In Eng.

Beauty and the Beast, collection Madame d'Aulnoy. Mankato: Creative Education, 1984. In Eng., Fr., Ger., Jap., and Sp.

La Petite Charlotte, by Henri Dès. Lausanne: Script & Mille-Pattes, 1986. In Fr.

On Ne Verra Jamais, by Henri Dès. Lausanne: Script & Mille-Pattes, 1986. In Fr.

Chanson Pour Mon Chien, by Henri Dès. Lausanne: Script & Mille-Pattes, 1986. In Fr.

The Poetical Pursuit of Food, by Sonoko Kondo. New York: Clarkson N. Potter, 1986. In Eng.

The Clicking of Cuthbert, by P. G. Wodehouse. Minneapolis: Redpath Press, 1986. In Eng.

The Lunatic's Tale, by Woody Allen. Minneapolis: Redpath Press, 1986. In Eng.

Baker's Bluejay Yarn, by Mark Twain. Minneapolis: Redpath Press, 1986. In Eng.

Taste, by Roald Dahl. Minneapolis: Redpath Press, 1986. In Eng.

A Wagner Matinee, by Willa Cather. Minneapolis: Redpath Press, 1986. In Eng.

The Gilded Six-bits, by Zora Neale Hurston. Minneapolis: Redpath Press, 1986. In Eng.

A & P, by John Updike. Minneapolis: Redpath Press, 1986. In Eng.

The Secret, by A. A. Milne. Minneapolis: Redpath Press, 1986. In Eng.

Mrs. Flowers, by Maya Angelou. Minneapolis: Redpath Press, 1986. In Eng.

Hour of Lead, by Anne Morrow Lindbergh. Minneapolis: Redpath Press, 1986. In Eng.

The Pheasant Hunter, by William Saroyan. Minneapolis: Redpath Press, 1986. In Eng.

Diary of a Newborn Baby, by Bob Greene. Minneapolis: Redpath Press, 1986. In Eng.

The Story-teller, by Saki. Minneapolis: Redpath Press, 1987. In Eng.

The Angel of the Bridge, by John Cheever. Minneapolis: Redpath Press, 1987. In Eng.

Christmas on the Roof of the World, by Ernest Hemingway. Minneapolis: Redpath Press, 1987. In Eng.

Zoo, by Ogden Nash. New York: Stewart, Tabori & Chang, 1987. In Eng.

Food, by Ogden Nash. New York: Stewart, Tabori & Chang, 1989. In Eng.

Books and Publications about Etienne Delessert

Les Dessins d'Etienne Delessert, by Jacques Chessex. Lausanne: Bertil Galland, 1974.

Musée des Arts Décoratifs, le Louvre. Catalogue. Paris: Musée des Arts Décoratifs, 1975.

Musée des Arts Décoratifs, Lausanne. Catalogue. Lausanne: Musée des Arts Décoratifs, 1976.

Images à la Page. Paris: Gallimard, 1984.

Something About the Author, Vol. 46. Edited by Anne Commire. Detroit: Gale Research Company, 1987.

Idea Magazine No. 66 (1964).

Idea Magazine No. 71 (1966).

Snyder, Jerome. Graphis Magazine No. 128, Zürich 1967.

Alexandre, Alexandre. Novum-Gebrauchsgraphik, Munich 1976.

Gallaz, Christophe. Graphis Magazine No. 208, Zürich 1980-81.

de Neve, Rose. Print Magazine March-April, New York 1991.

Danish (Dan.), Dutch (Dut.), English (Eng.), French (Fr.), Greek (Gr.), Hebrew (Heb.), Italian (It.), Japanese (Jap.), Persian (Per.), Portuguese (Port.), Spanish (Sp.)

Acknowledgments

▲ We all know that a single word is worth a thousand pictures, so I would like to use a few of them to acknowledge Andy Stewart at Stewart, Tabori & Chang and Pierre Marchand at Editions Gallimard for initiating this book; Leslie Stoker for her guiding hand; Ann Campbell in New York and Marion Challier in Paris for their editorial talents; and Kathy Rosenbloom for her inspired supervision of the production of this beautiful book. My gratitude goes to the friends who portrayed me so well in their essays. And thank you, Rita, for your stoic patience in the selection of the images and for the staging of the pages in your classic and elegant style.   E . D .

Contributors

■ Bertil Galland is a journalist, author, and publisher in Lausanne. For twenty years his house, Editions Bertil Galland, has published the writers who gave Swiss French literature its international standing.

■ Yves Beccaria is the director-general of Bayard Presse in Paris—one of the preeminent publishers of magazines for children and adults. He has originated the majority of its titles within the last thirty years.

■ Judy Garlan has been art director at The Atlantic Monthly since 1981. Previously she art directed five other magazines, including Art News, Crawdaddy, and Cue, spent two years designing for a small New York advertising agency, and served as a special design consultant for Time magazine.

■ Since 1949, Janine Despinette has worked for the promotion of children's literature through writing, publishing, and active participation in international organizations such as IBBY and UNESCO. She is a juror for major international children's literature competitions.

■ David Macaulay is the head of the illustration department at the Rhode Island School of Design and has been creating books since 1973. Among them are Cathedral, Unbuilding, and Underground from his highly original architecture series, Black and White, the 1991 Caldecott Medal winner, and the international bestseller The Way Things Work.

■ Antonio Faeti was born in 1939. He now teaches the history of children's literature at the University of Bologna. Also as author, painter, and columnist, Faeti is an expert in the interpretation of comics, illustration, and imagery.

Designed by Rita Marshall
Composed in Berner and Caslon 471
by Printing Prep Inc., Buffalo, New York
Printed and bound by
Toppan Printing Company, Ltd., Tokyo, Japan